T0393352

WHERE AM I?

In the Arctic

Written by Noah Leatherland

Enslow
PUBLISHING

Published in 2025 by Enslow Publishing, LLC
2544 Clinton Street
Buffalo, NY 14224

© 2024 BookLife Publishing Ltd.

Written by:
Noah Leatherland

Edited by:
Rebecca Phillips-Bartlett

Designed by:
Amy Li

Cataloging-in-Publication Data

Names: Leatherland, Noah, 1999-.
Title: In the arctic / Noah Leatherland.
Description: Buffalo, NY : Enslow Publishing, 2025. | Series: Where am I? | Includes glossary.
Identifiers: ISBN 9781978541689 (pbk.) | ISBN 9781978541696 (library bound) | ISBN 9781978541702 (ebook)
Subjects: LCSH: Animals--Arctic regions--Juvenile literature.Habitat (Ecology)--Arctic regions--Juvenile literature.
Classification: LCC QL105.L38 2025 | DDC 591.9989--dc23

Manufactured in the United States of America

CPSIA compliance information: Batch #CW25ENS: For further information contact Enslow Publishing LLC at 1-800-398-2504.

Please visit our website, www.enslowpublishing.com. For a free color catalog of all our high-quality books, call toll free 1-800-398-2504 or fax 1-877-980-4454.

Find us on

PHOTO CREDITS All images are courtesy of Shutterstock.com, unless otherwise specified. With thanks to Getty Images, Thinkstock Photo and iStockphoto.
Recurring – Tartila, Leonid Ikan, Volha Valadzionak, Chinch, inspiring.team. Cover – Jennifer G. Lang, Jim Cumming. 2–3 – Cavan-Images. 4–5 – Gregory A. Pozhvanov, CherylRamalho, Katharine Moore. 6–7 – Vaclav Sebek, StockSmartStart. 8–9 – COULANGES, e-leet, lattesmile. 10–11 – Tanya Klim, StockSmartStart. 12–13 – evgenii mitroshin, Paul Loewen, StockSmartStart. 14–15 – ecoventurestravel, Fitawoman, StockSmartStart. 16–17 – adamikarl, AndreAnita, FloridaStock, Andrew Krasovitckii. 18–19 – Valeriy Karpeev, Maquiladora. 20–21 – Dave McKissick, Nick Pecker, NotionPic. 22–23 – Jim Cumming, Jukka Jantunen.

CONTENTS

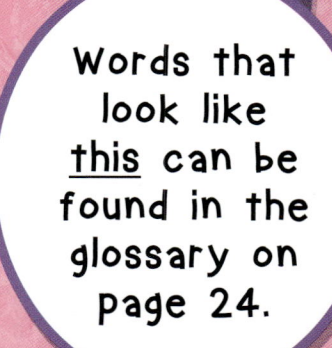

Words that look like this can be found in the glossary on page 24.

WHERE AM I?

Welcome to the Arctic! The Arctic surrounds the North Pole. A lot of the Arctic is called the <u>tundra</u>. Other parts of the Arctic are made of large patches of ice floating in the sea.

TUNDRA

SEA ICE

4

Many animals find their homes in Arctic habitats. Some animals hide from <u>predators</u> to stay alive. Some predators hide to help them sneak up on their <u>prey</u>.

A habitat is where an animal lives and has everything they need to survive.

POLAR BEAR

I am a polar bear. I am the top predator in the Arctic. My fur works as <u>camouflage</u> to help me blend into the white snow and ice of my habitat. However, my fur is not actually white!

I have <u>hollow</u> fur. When light hits my fur, it makes the fur look white. I also have black skin. My black nose can help you spot me hiding on the ice.

Can you spot me?

HARP SEAL

I am a harp seal. Harp seals like me have soft white fur when we are young. Our fur camouflages us with the Arctic snow and ice. This camouflage helps young harp seals stay safe from predators while we are on the ice.

As harp seals like me get older, we go into the water more. We <u>shed</u> our fluffy white coat and grow a gray one. The darker coat is hard to see underwater and by rocks.

Can you see my body under the water?

9

SNOWY OWL

I am a snowy owl. Many birds make their nests high up in trees. However, in much of the Arctic, there are very few trees. Snowy owls like me are some of the only birds that nest on the ground.

I am a <u>patient</u> hunter. I find a high perch where I can watch for prey. When I spot something, I quickly swoop down and snatch it with my long claws, called talons.

Can you see me perched in the tree?

11

ARCTIC HARE

I am an Arctic hare. I have a white fur coat. This helps me camouflage and hide from predators. I am a very fast runner. Even if a predator spots me, it is hard for them to keep up with me.

As well as camouflaging me in the snow, my fur keeps me warm. If I need to warm myself up, I find other hares and we huddle together.

How many Arctic hares can you see?

ARCTIC FOX

I am an Arctic fox. I have white fur to hide from predators and my prey. However, sometimes I let other animals hunt for me. Sometimes, I follow polar bears and eat food they leave behind.

In some parts of the Arctic, the ice and snow melt away in the summer. White fur is not always helpful. I shed my white coat and grow a darker one in the summer.

Why would a dark coat not be good in winter?

15

PTARMIGAN

I am a ptarmigan. I am a bird that has <u>adapted</u> to life in the Arctic. I have feathers on my legs and feet. This helps me keep warm and also helps me walk on the snow.

FEATHERY FEET

I change my feathers with the seasons. In the winter, I have white feathers to match the snow. In summer, I have brown and gray feathers to match the ground.

Which feathers are for winter? Which feathers are for summer?

17

BELUGA WHALE

I am a beluga whale. We are some of the noisiest creatures in the sea. We <u>communicate</u> with each other using whistles, clicks, chirps, and more. We often work together to hunt our prey.

Beluga whales like me have gray or white skin. This helps us blend in with the ice that floats in the Arctic Ocean. When we poke our heads out, it can look like a lump of ice!

Can you see me?

LEMMING

I am a lemming. I am a little furry creature that can be found all over the Arctic. I have a lot of predators because I am so small. I <u>rely</u> on the snow to keep me safe.

I dig into the snow and live in tunnels. These tunnels help me hide from predators. Although snow is cold, having lots of snow above me keeps me warm.

Can you see me peeking out of my tunnel?

21

HIDING IN THE HABITAT

Staying hidden and out of sight is very important for many animals. It can help them stay safe from predators or it can help them hunt their prey.

ARCTIC WOLVES BLENDING IN WITH THE SNOW

All over the world, different animals hide and use camouflage to help them survive. You might be able to see some of them… but they are really good at hiding!

AN ARCTIC GROUND SQUIRREL HIDING UNDERGROUND

GLOSSARY

ADAPTED	changed over time to suit the environment
CAMOUFLAGE	the ability to blend in with the surroundings
COMMUNICATE	to pass information between two or more things
HOLLOW	containing an empty space inside
PATIENT	happy to wait calmly for something
PREDATORS	animals that hunt other animals for food
PREY	animals that are hunted by other animals for food
RELY	to need something for support
SHED	to remove and replace something with another one that has grown underneath
TUNDRA	cold, flat land where no trees are able to grow

INDEX

24